To:
Daniel
from: Grams
1991

THE LOST SHEEP

Regine Schindler

illustrated by
Hilde Heyduck-Huth

ABINGDON

Nashville

Daniel has one hundred sheep. He lives in a small village in faraway Palestine. Only in winter, after the fields have been harvested, are the sheep allowed to graze close to the houses. Every spring Daniel goes away with his sheep and returns in the fall. He carries a cloth bag and a slingshot. Daniel also carries a thick stick called a staff. He uses the stick to protect himself from the wild animals that might try to steal a sheep.

Daniel sets out early in the morning. He knows a little valley where fresh grass grows and where there is a spring. By afternoon he is there. All the sheep are with him. He counts them again and again. Whenever one gets behind, Daniel calls it to him. He knows all their names, and the sheep know his voice.

Daniel lets the sheep graze and leads them to the spring where they can drink. Daniel is happy. Many shepherds know about this good place, but none of them is here today.

Now Daniel has to find a resting place for his animals. They cannot move on because the old ones and little ones are tired. Daniel drives the sheep into a cave so they will be protected from the wind. In front of the cave

he builds a fire. The fire not only warms him, but it keeps the wild animals away. Daniel lies beside the fire with his slingshot and staff next to him.

The next morning Daniel moves on. Soon it becomes very hot. He wraps his big shepherd's scarf around his head to keep out the burning heat. Sometimes Daniel is afraid of the sun because there are no trees or shade where he can rest. Only dry thorn bushes grow in the desert and small patches of green grass. Then the sheep plug the grass and chew it with their teeth until Daniel drives them on. He must again find a watering place.

Daniel must find another sleeping place and build a fire for his sheep. Today he brings his animals to a pen. Rocks are stacked on top of each other in a circle to make a low wall. The animals spend the night inside the wall and cannot run away.

Daniel can keep lookout over the wall. He can hear the faithful shepherd dog bark, he is not afraid. As it grows dark he wraps himself in his warm coat.

The next day they move on to find fresh grass. Many more days pass. Often the way is very steep. Daniel has to lead his sheep through a deep canyon and then up the other side. The rocks are hard. A big old sheep is injured, and Daniel must help it. In his bag he carries healing herbs. Daniel must stay with his flock in a pen for many days until the big old sheep is well. Luckily, there are water and good plants around.

Daniel moves on through the desert, over cliffs and mountains. He is tired when he counts his sheep in the evening, but he must make sure all of his sheep are with him. Daniel feels fortunate and thinks, "It is a good summer!"

One hot noon Daniel gives his sheep a rest. The animals drink, and Daniel counts them. Has he made a mistake? He counts them again. One sheep is missing, a small one named Azo. "Azo," Daniel calls out, "Azo, Azo," he shouts as loud as he can. "Azo, Azo," softly echo the cliff walls. The sheep bleat. Azo is gone, and Daniel is afraid. He knows he has to find the little one before it is dark. He drives the other sheep into a cave. He lights a fire and says to his dog, "Stay here! Sit!" Sadly the dog wags his tail. He would like to go with his master.

Daniel hurries back over the rocks and sand dunes. Again and again he shouts, "Azo," as he climbs up the mountain. Maybe the little one is there. Daniel knows Azo likes to climb. So he climbs higher and higher. It is very dangerous, and sometimes he must hold fast to a rock jutting out or jump over a deep crevice. "Azo, Azo, are you there?"

Finally, a faint "Baa, baa" answers back. Daniel finds the little sheep in a thick, thorny bush. Azo kicks, he twists around, but he cannot get free. Daniel takes a knife and cuts the thorn bush away to free little Azo.

He picks Azo up in his arms and strokes him. Daniel is happy that he has found the little lost sheep. The way back to the flock is difficult. Daniel places the sheep on his shoulders. It is already evening and only the moon shines, but Daniel finds the way. He knows where the cave is with the other ninety-nine sheep. He sees no fire. It has gone out because Daniel has left the flock alone for so long. But nothing has happened to them. They stand close to one another because they are afraid and cold.

The fall is near, and Daniel wants to return quickly to his village with his sheep. He is happy! He wants to tell everything to his friends. He wants to tell everyone, "I have found my sheep that was lost high up in the mountains." All the way back home, Daniel carries the small sheep Azo.

When Daniel returns to his village, the children run to him. Then grown-ups surround him, too. "The little one here, Azo, was lost. He climbed high up in the mountains. And I have found him. I am happy! Rejoice with me." Daniel invites everyone in the village to his house to celebrate. His small house is completely full. Everyone laughs and is happy. They join hands. They sing and dance. Daniel the shepherd is very happy. He rejoices over the sheep that was once lost but is now found.

This story comes from a parable in the Bible. Jesus said that just as the shepherd cares for his sheep, so God cares for us. The shepherd searches for every sheep that is lost. This is how God cares for us. He rejoices over each one he finds.

Like the shepherd searching for his animal,
so, dear God, search for me.
I cannot go astray.
God, you will always see me.
You carry me safe in your arms.
There I am happy; there I am warm.